Recipe Hacks

for

Ramen

Instant Noodles

Introduction

In these tough economic times, it is important to find ways to save money, especially when feeding your family. Maybe you are a college student looking to save money by taking a break from fast food or paying at the cafeteria. Maybe you are a parent with a large family to feed or maybe you are just thrifty and need to find creative ways to save money without sacrificing flavor!

This recipe book contains tons of tasty and creative hacks that go beyond the traditional with delicious options such as adding vegetables, cheese, meats and other seasonings. They can be sprinkled dry in salads, casseroles and wraps and much, much more.

Ramen instant noodles may be cheap but they don't have to be boring if you know how to Hack it!

Ramen Mac and Cheese

Ingredients:

4 (3 oz.) pkgs. of Ramen noodles (noodles only)
1 tbsp. butter
1 tbsp. flour
1½ cups milk
1 (8 oz.) package Pepper Jack Cheese, shredded (2 cups)
2 tsps. Sriracha sauce
½ tsp. salt

Directions:

1. Bring a pot of water to boil and add noodles.
2. Boil 1 minute, or 1 minute 15 seconds.
3. Drain in a colander and rinse with cold water. Spray a little oil and toss them around with your hands breaking them up. (I left them right in the colander.)
4. Heat butter in a large saucepan on medium heat and add flour to make a roux.
5. Cook about a minute.
6. Pour in the milk and cook until it becomes frothy and thick, stir occasionally.
7. Reduce heat to low and gradually add cheese.
8. Add Sriracha and salt and stir until cheese is melted.
9. Increase heat to medium to medium/low and add noodles.
10. Cook until heated through, about 1-2 minutes.
11. Add milk a tbsp. at a time if you want the sauce to be thinner.

Kimchi Ramen

Ingredients:

1 tbsp. vegetable oil
5 shiitake mushrooms, thinly sliced
½ cup cabbage kimchi, chopped
¼ cup kimchi juice
2½ cups chicken or vegetable stock
2 tsps. Korean red pepper powder (gochugaru)
¼ tsp. sugar
1 tsp. sesame oil
1 package instant noodles
1 scallion, julienned

Directions:

1. In a medium pot, add the vegetable oil and the mushrooms.
2. Stir-fry for 3 minutes.
3. Add the kimchi and stir-fry for another 2 minutes.
4. Add the kimchi juice, stock, korean red pepper powder, sugar, and sesame oil.
5. Bring to a boil and simmer for 5 minutes.
6. Meanwhile, open up your package of instant noodles.
7. Discard the flavor packet, and boil the noodles according to the package instructions. Transfer the cooked noodles to a bowl.
8. Pour your broth over the noodles, and serve with scallions on top!

Sriracha Ramen Noodle Soup

Ingredients:

2 tbsps. sesame oil
2 tbsps. sriracha hot sauce
1 small onion, diced
1 small roma tomato, diced
1 tbsp. ginger, grated
5 cloves garlic, minced
1/2 tsp. garlic powder
1/2 tsp. celery salt
4 cups vegetable broth
2 cups water
1 tbsp. soy sauce
1 tsp. rice vinegar (optional; only if you like tang)
3 pkgs. ramen noodles
1/2 cup scallions, chopped
1/2 cup cilantro, chopped
2 poached eggs (optional)

Directions:

1. Add the sesame oil and sriracha to a large stockpot and bring to a simmer over medium-heat.
2. Add the onion and tomato and cook for 4 minutes, stirring occasionally.
3. Add the ginger, garlic, and seasonings.
4. Cook for 2 minutes or until fragrant.
5. Add 2 cups of water and transfer mixture to a blender or food processor and pulse until smooth.
6. Return mixture to the pot and add the broth.
7. Bring to a simmer; add soy sauce and vinegar (if using), and simmer for 8-10 minutes. Taste and adjust seasoning as needed.

8. Add the ramen noodles to the broth and simmer for an additional 2-3 minutes, or until the noodles have softened.
9. Add the scallions, stir to combine.
10. Remove pan from heat, ladle soup into bowls, and top with cilantro and eggs.

Spicy Korean Chili Dressing Ramen

Ingredients:

1 brick of ramen noodles (discard the seasoning packet)
1 tbsp. Spicy Korean Chili Seasoning
1 tbsp. soy sauce
½ tbsp.. sesame oil
1 tsp rice vinegar
½ tsp honey or agave nectar
1 green onion, green part only, chopped

Directions:

1. Cook the ramen noodles according to package instructions.
2. Drain the noodles and run cold water over them to stop the cooking process.
3. Combine the Spicy Korean Chili Seasoning, soy sauce, sesame oil, rice vinegar and honey/agave.
4. Whisk to mix thoroughly, then toss with the noodles.

Ramen Chicken Salad

Ingredients:

1/2 head of cabbage, shredded
3 large carrots, shredded
4-5 green onions, chopped
1/2 red or green bell pepper (optional)
2 pkgs. of chicken flavored ramen noodles, seasoning packets reserved
2 cup cooked and shredded chicken (optional)
1/2 cup slivered almonds

Dressing Ingredients:

2/3 cup vegetable oil
6 tbsp. rice vinegar
2 tbsp. low-sodium soy sauce
1/4 cup white sugar
2 chicken flavored ramen seasoning pkgs.

Directions:

1. In a large bowl mix together cabbage, carrots, onion, chicken, and almonds.
2. Remove the seasoning packets from the ramen noodle pkgs. and set aside for use in the dressing.
3. Place noodles in a large ziplock bag and crush them with a rolling pin.
4. Add the noodles to the bowl with the cabbage.
5. Mix dressing ingredients together.
6. Pour desired amount of dressing over salad and toss to combine.
7. Serve immediately.

Cherry Tomato Ramen Noodle Bowl

Vinaigrette Ingredients:

1 heaping tsp. lemon zest (from about one large lemon)
2 tsps. minced lemon basil (or 1 1/2 tsps. sweet basil)
2 tbsps. lemon juice (from large lemon or two small)
2 tbsps. white wine vinegar
2 tbsps. extra virgin olive oil
1 tbsp. honey or agave
1/2 tsp. kosher salt (plus more as necessary, to taste)

Noodle Bowl Ingredients:

3 pkgs. ramen noodles, flavor packets discarded
1 tbsp. extra virgin olive oil
1 avocado, diced
1 pint cherry tomatoes, sliced into disks or quartered wedges
1 tbsp. lemon basil or sweet basil, minced

Directions:

1. Add all ingredients to a small mixing bowl and whisk well.
2. Set aside for at least a half hour, if possible, to let the flavors meld.
3. Taste, and add more salt if needed, one pinch at a time.
4. Bring a medium pot of water to boil.
5. Add the ramen noodles and reduce heat slightly to maintain an active simmer without boiling over.
6. Cook for three minutes (or according to package directions).
7. Drain in a colander and set aside to cool to room temperature (this takes just a few minutes).

8. When the ramen noodles have cooled, toss them with one tbsp. of olive oil plus two tbsps. of the vinaigrette.
9. Divide the noodles evenly between two entree-sized bowls.
10. Top each bowl with half of the sliced tomatoes and avocados, and drizzle the remaining vinaigrette evenly over each. Garnish with minced basil.

Ramen Noodle Stir Fry

Sauce Ingredients:

1 tbsp. rice vinegar
1 tbsp. toasted sesame oil
2 tbsps. soy sauce
2 tsps. hoisin sauce
1 tsp. brown sugar
1 tsp. minced garlic
1 tsp. minced ginger

Stir Fry Ingredients:

9 oz. ramen noodles, about 3 packs (discard the flavor packet)
1 tbsp. peanut oil (or other high-heat oil)
1 tsp. minced garlic
1 tsp. minced ginger
4 oz. shiitake mushrooms, stems removed, sliced
1 small head of broccoli, cut into florets and sliced julienne
1/2 red bell pepper, sliced julienne
1 egg, lightly scrambled (optional)
2 scallions, sliced
1 tbsp. minced cilantro

Directions:

1. Whisk the sauce ingredients together in a bowl and set aside.
2. Bring a medium pot of water to boil over high heat, and cook the noodles according to package directions.
3. Meanwhile, heat the oil in a large skillet or wok over medium-high heat until shimmering.
4. Add the garlic, ginger, mushrooms, broccoli, and peppers, and sauté for about a minute.

5. Add the scrambled egg, if using, and stir until it's mostly set up.
6. Mix in with the vegetables.
7. Add the noodles, and, if desired, use scissors to snip the long strands into more fork-manageable lengths. Drizzle the sauce over the stir fry, plus a big pinch of cilantro, and mix well.
8. Garnish with scallions and more cilantro before serving.

Italian Ramen Noodles

Ingredients:

2 cups water
3 tbsps. butter
1 tbsp. olive oil
2 cups Parmesan cheese
1 tbsp. black pepper
2 pkgs. instant ramen (minus the seasoning packets)
1 handful oyster mushrooms (optional)

Directions:

1. Combine water, butter and olive oil in a saucepan and bring it to a boil.
2. Stir often and reduce heat to medium before adding the cheese and black pepper.
3. Add the instant ramen and continue to stir so that the cheese doesn't clump up.
4. If there is too much liquid for the ramen to absorb, pour some out.
5. Once the noodles are cooked and the liquid has reduced, the dish is ready. You want the sauce to coat the back of a spoon.
6. Serve immediately and eat as soon as possible. Bonus: quickly stir-fry some oyster mushrooms on the side to convince yourself it's healthy.

Cheddar Broccoli Ramen

Ingredients:

2 Packets of Rice-a-Roni Cheddar Broccoli powder mix
Ramen
Water

Directions:

1. Microwave your Ramen in a bowl for around 3:45 min.
2. Once it's done, pour in the two powder mix packets and stir.
3. Let it sit for a few minutes to allow the liquid to absorb in to the noodles.

Ramen Chili

Ingredients:

1 can spicy beef and bean chili
Ramen
Water
Grated cheese, optional
Extra chili powder, optional

Directions:

1. Microwave Ramen in a bowl for around 3:45 min.
2. Pour in the powder mix packet and stir.
3. Take out the excess water and pour in to the chili.
4. Add cheese or add extra chili powder if desired.

Ramen Chicken Soup

Ingredients:

1 pkg. Ramen instant noodles, any flavor (seasoning
packets discarded)
1 can creamy chicken soup
Water.

Directions:

1. Microwave your Ramen in a bowl for around 3:45 min.
2. Once it's done, pour in the two powder mix packets and
   stir.
3. Take out the excess water.
4. Make the soup according to the directions on the can.
5. Add the creamy chicken soup to the noodles.

Ramen Fudge Desert

Ingredients:

1 pkg. Ramen instant noodles, any flavor (seasoning packets discarded)
1 cup brown sugar
1 tsp. vanilla extract
1 cup chocolate syrup
Powdered sugar
Whipped cream

Directions:

1. Cook ramen as directed on package, but instead of adding seasoning, add a cup of brown sugar.
2. Pour out most of the water and add vanilla extract and chocolate syrup.
3. Sprinkle on powdered sugar.
4. Add whipped cream.

Ramen Potato Soup

Ingredients:

1 can cream of potato soup
¼ cup shredded cheddar cheese
1 russet potato, diced
2 slices bacon, chopped
2 green onions, thinly sliced

Directions:

1. Fry bacon in saucepan until crisp.
2. Remove and let cool on paper towel for 5 minutes.
3. Discard bacon fat from saucepan.
4. Wash and peel potato. Dice into small, bite-sized pieces.
5. Cook potato in saucepan until brown, about 10 minutes.
6. Add potato soup and cook over medium heat for about 6 minutes.
7. Ladle soup into two serving bowls and sprinkle with cheese, bacon and scallions.

Ramen Snack Mix

Ingredients:

Chicken flavored Ramen noodles with season packets
retained
Chex cereal
Pretzel sticks
Nuts

Directions:

1. Break up the Ramen noodles
2. Mix ramen pieces with Chex cereal, pretzel sticks and nuts.
3. Sprinkle the sauce packet over the snacks.
4. Mix well.
5. Serve and enjoy.

Ramen Noodle Bake

Ingredients:

1 pkg. Ramen instant noodles, beef flavor (seasoning packet reserved)
3 pkgs. Ramen instant noodles, any flavor (seasoning packets discarded)
1 (26 oz.) jar spaghetti sauce
1 lb. cooked ground beef or Italian sausage
2 cups mozzarella cheese, divided
3 1/2 cups water

Directions:

1. Preheat oven to 400 degrees.
2. Break up ramen noodles into a greased 9 x 13 inch pan.
3. They should cover the bottom of the dish.
4. Sprinkle the cooked meat over dry noodles.
5. Pour the jar of sauce over the top.
6. Sprinkle the beef flavor packet over the sauce.
7. Sprinkle one cup of the cheese over the top of sauce.
8. Gently mix together.
9. Pour the water over the top.
10. Cover tightly with aluminum foil and bake 40 to 50 minutes or until liquid is totally absorbed.
11. Remove from oven and remove foil.
12. Sprinkle the remaining cheese over the top.
13. Return to oven for 5- 10 minutes until the cheese is melted and bubbly.

Ramen Broccoli Casserole

Ingredients:

1/2 cup mayonnaise
1/2 cup plain yogurt
1 1/4 cup shredded sharp cheddar cheese
1/3 cup blue cheese dressing
2 eggs
1/2 tsp. salt
1 1/2 tsp. fresh ground black pepper
Flavor Pack from Ramen
6 cups broccoli, peeled stems and heads, chopped and blanched in salted water
12 oz. sliced mushrooms, Sautéed in 1 tbsp. butter
1 pkg. chicken flavored Ramen noodles, broken up

Directions:

1. Preheat oven to 350 degrees F.
2. In a bowl combine mayonnaise, yogurt, cheddar cheese, blue cheese dressing, eggs, salt, pepper, and flavor pack from noodles.
3. In a separate bowl combine broccoli, mushrooms, and broken noodles then toss together wet mixture and vegetables to evenly coat.
4. Place in an 8 by 8-inch baking dish that has been sprayed with non- stick cooking spray and cook for 45 minutes covered.
5. Then remove cover and bake for additional 15 minutes to brown.
6. Cool for 15 minutes before serving.

Spicy Thai Green Curry Ramen

Ingredients:

2 tbsp. coconut oil or peanut oil
Green curry paste
4 small green Thai chilies
1/2 cup shallot, diced
4 cloves garlic, minced
2 thumb-size pieces ginger, grated
3 tbsp. lemongrass
1/2 tsp. ground white pepper
2 tbsp. fish sauce
3 tsp. brown sugar
2 tbsp. lime juice
Salt to taste
1 small onion, large diced
2 cups carrots, large diced
2 cups oyster mushroom, large diced
1/2 can coconut milk
1/2 can water
1 tsp. grated lime zest
1 pkg. ramen noodles
1 cup bean sprouts, washed
2 radishes, washed and thinly sliced
1/2 cup red onion, thinly sliced
Generous handful fresh Thai basil and cilantro, washed and dried

Directions:

1. Place a large pot over medium-high heat.
2. Add the oil and swirl around, then add curry paste, chiles, shallots, garlic, ginger and lemon grass and diced onion. Sauté until fragrant, about 2-3 minutes.

3. Add coconut milk and water.
4. Bring curry to a boil and reduce to a slight simmer.
5. Add the carrots.
6. Cover and allow to simmer for 5 minutes.
7. Stir occasionally.
8. Meanwhile bring a medium pot of water to a boil. This will be your cooking water for the ramen.
9. Place ramen into boiling water and loosen the noodles, making sure they are evenly distributed.
10. Cook ramen according to package directions.
11. Drain and rinse under cold water.
12. Set aside.
13. Add oyster mushrooms, lime zest, white pepper, and brown sugar to curry, stirring well to incorporate.
14. Simmer another 5-10 minutes and add fish sauce and lime juice.
15. Salt to taste and adjust flavors to your liking - adding more fish sauce to make it saltier, more sugar for sweetness, lime for acid and if it's too spicy you can temper it with more coconut milk.
16. Place ramen into curry and turn off heat.
17. Divide into bowls and garnish with fresh herbs, bean sprouts and shaved radish.

Ramen Noodle Pancakes

Pancake Ingredients:

1 pkg. (3 oz.) Ramen noodles, any flavor
1 medium zucchini, shredded
2 scallions (green onions), finely sliced
1 medium carrot, shredded
2 large eggs, beaten
2 tbsp. flour
1 tbsp. lemon juice
2-3 tbsp. oil, divided

Sauce Ingredients:

3 tbsp. soy sauce
3tbsp. rice vinegar
Pinch red pepper flakes (optional)

Directions:

1. Mix together soy sauce, vinegar, and red pepper flakes.
2. Break up the ramen noodles, into 4 sections.
3. Reserve the seasoning packet. Cook according to direction with one exception.
4. Boil for 2 minutes only.
5. Drain.
6. Place cooked noodles in a medium mixing bowl, add shredded zucchini and carrot, scallions, flour, and seasoning packet.
7. Stir well.
8. In a non-stick skillet, heat oil over medium-high heat.
9. Using 1/3 cup measure, place noodle mix in cup, and press down lightly with a spoon.
10. Place noodles in frying pan, press down slightly with a spatula, to help the pancake hold together.
11. Fry 2-3 minutes on each side.

12. Repeat steps using remaining oil as needed.

Ramen Grilled Cheese

Ingredients
½ package of ramen, any "flavor"
½ of the ramen seasoning packet (discard oil packet and dried vegetable packet.)
1 handful of kimchi, chopped and squeezed of excess kimchi "juice"
1 tbsps. oil for cooking
2 tbsp. butter, softened
2 thick slices very sturdy bread
1 handful of mozzarella or jack cheese
1 handful American or Cheddar cheese

Directions:

1. Bring a pot of water to a boil over high heat.
2. Drop the ramen noodles in and cook until the ramen noodles are soft, about 8 minutes.
3. Drain the ramen noodles of the cooking liquid using a colander, then put the noodles back into the pot or into a bowl.
4. Pour the contents of half the seasoning packet over the noodles.
5. Toss the noodles to combine.
6. Set aside to prepare sandwich.
7. Heat olive oil in a frying pan over low heat.
8. Spread the outside of both slices of bread with softened butter.
9. Place both slices of bread buttered-side down in the oil in the pan. Pile one slice with mozzarella/jack cheese; pile the other slice of bread with American/Cheddar cheese.
10. Cook until bread is toasted and cheese has melted.
11. Remove the grilled bread with cheese to a plate or cutting board. Pile as much ramen noodles on one slice of the bread as you'd like.

12. Add chopped kimchi on top.
13. Close the sandwich with the other slice of grilled bread and cheese. Press together firmly.

Ramen Pizza

Ingredients:

2 pkgs. instant ramen noodles, noodles only
3 tbsps. extra-virgin olive oil
12 oz. grated mozzarella or Jack cheese
3/4 cup homemade or store-bought pizza sauce
2 oz. grated parmesan cheese, divided
Toppings, as desired

Directions:

1. Adjust oven rack to center position and preheat oven to 450 degrees F.
2. Bring a large pot of salted water to a boil.
3. Add noodles and cook, breaking them apart with tongs, until flexible but not completely softened, about 2 minutes.
4. Drain carefully.
5. Heat olive oil in a 10-inch cast iron skillet over medium heat until shimmering.
6. Add noodles and press with the bottom of a spatula into an even later that completely covers the bottom of the skillet.
7. Reduce heat to low.
8. Spread half of mozzarella or Jack cheese evenly over noodles, then spread sauce, going all the way to the edge of the pan.
9. Spread remaining mozzarella or jack on top along with half of parmesan.
10. Top pizza as desired, then place in oven.
11. Bake until top is browned and bubbly, about 20 minutes.

12. Sprinkle with remaining parmesan. Allow to cool slightly, then use a thin metal spatula to loosen edges from skillet.
13. Carefully slide pizza out onto cutting board.
14. Slice, and serve immediately.

Ramen Meat Loaf

1 pkg. beef flavor Top Ramen
1/4 cup onion, chopped
1/4 cup celery, chopped
3 tbsp. parsley, chopped
1 (8 oz.) can tomato sauce
2 eggs, beaten
1 1/2 lbs. lean ground beef

Directions:

1. Before opening, break up Ramen noodles into small pieces and combine in a mixing bowl with the seasonings from the flour packet, onion, celery, parsley, tomato sauce, and eggs.
2. Stir together and mix in ground beef. Shape into a firm loaf in a buttered loaf pan.
3. Bake at 375 degrees for 50 to 60 minutes.
4. Cool for 12 minutes before serving.
5. Serves 6.

Ramen Slaw

Slaw Ingredients:

1/2 head shredded cabbage, green or red
4 green onions, chopped
1/2 cup toasted almond slivers
2 tsp. sesame seeds
1 pkg. Ramen noodles, chicken flavor

Slaw Directions:

1. Mix all ingredients together except Ramen noodles.
2. Add dressing (see below) and refrigerate.
3. Break up noodles and add right before serving.

Dressing Ingredients:

1/2 cup oil
2 tbsp. sugar
3 tbsp. vinegar
Ramen chicken flavor seasoning packet

Dressing Directions:

1. Mix all dressing ingredients together and pour over
   slaw.

Broccoli Ramen Slaw

Ingredients:

1 pkg. broccoli slaw
1 cup slivered almonds
1 cup sunflower seeds
1 cup green onion
2 pkg. beef Ramen noodle seasoning
1 cup vegetable oil
1/3 cup vinegar
1/2 cup sugar

Directions:

1. Mix together first 4 ingredients and let stand overnight.
2. Mix beef Ramen noodle seasoning with vegetable oil, vinegar and sugar. One-half hour before serving, crumble up noodles.
3. Add to slaw mixture and stir.
4. Stir the dressing mixture well and add to slaw.

Cabbage Ramen Salad

4 cup shredded cabbage, (red or green)
1 pkg. Ramen noodles, (chicken), broken or crushed
1 1/2 cup slivered almonds
3 tbsp. sesame seeds
3 tbsp. white vinegar
1 tsp. Dijon mustard
2 tbsp. sugar
1/4 tsp. pepper
1/2 cup salad oil
2 tbsp. fresh cilantro, (or 1 tsp. dried)

Directions:

1. Toast the almonds and sesame seeds in a little butter, set aside.
2. Dressing: Take the seasoning pack from the noodles and mix with the oil, vinegar, sugar, pepper, mustard and cilantro. Just before serving, combine the cabbage, noodles (raw), almonds and sesame seeds.
3. Pour on dressing and toss well.

Peanut Ramen Cabbage Salad

Ingredients:

1 pkg. Ramen, oriental or chicken flavor
1/2 sm. head cabbage, chopped
2 or 3 scallions, chopped
1/4 - 1/2 cup peanuts

Dressing Ingredients:

1/4 cup oil
Flavor packet from the Ramen

Directions:

1. Cook noodles as directed, drain, rinse in cool water.
2. Add flavor packet to water and dissolve; then add water to oil.
3. Let set awhile.
4. Toss everything together.
5. Serve and enjoy!

Ramen Supreme

Ingredients:

4 pkg. cooked chicken flavored Ramen (do not add seasoning packets until after draining)
2 pkgs. frozen chopped spinach, cooked and drained
1 cube butter
1 lg. carton sour cream
1 lb. grated Jack or Monterey cheese

Directions:

1. Mix all ingredients in a 9x13 baking pan.
2. Bake at 350 degrees for 35 minutes.
3. Serve and enjoy!

Tex-Mex Ramen

Ingredients:

1 pkg. beef flavored Ramen noodles
1/2 lb. ground beef
1/2 tsp. Mexican seasonings or chili powder

Directions:

1. Before opening, break-up noodles in package.
2. Add noodles to one cup boiling water.
3. Cook uncovered, stir occasionally for 3 minutes.
4. Rinse and drain well.
5. Cook 1/2 pound ground beef with seasonings from flavor packet and 1/2 tsp. Mexican seasonings (or chili powder) until meat is browned.
6. Arrange meat over hot noodles.
7. Top with your choice of shredded cheese, shredded lettuce, taco sauce, sour cream (optional), avocado slices.

Peanut Ramen Noodle Salad

Ingredients:

2 package ramen noodles (any flavor)
½ cup Peanut Butter
¼ cup each water, vinegar and teriyaki sauce
½ tsp. minced garlic
¼ tsp. crushed red pepper flakes (optional)
1 cucumber, quartered lengthwise
2 carrots
2 scallions

Directions:

1. Bring 4 cups water to a boil in a medium saucepan.
2. Add ramen noodles (save seasoning packets for another use or discard).
3. Boil 3 minutes or until tender.
4. Drain and rinse under cold water; drain again.
5. Whisk peanut butter, water, vinegar, teriyaki sauce, garlic and crushed red pepper in a medium bowl until smooth.
6. Add noodles, cucumber, carrots and scallions.
7. Toss to mix and coat.

Asian Ramen Noodles with Shrimp

Ingredients:

1 can lite coconut milk
2 cup preshredded carrots
1 medium onion
12 oz. raw medium shrimp
2 package shrimp-flavor ramen noodles (reserve 1 seasoning packet)
4 oz. snow peas
1/4 cup finely chopped cilantro
4 tsp. fresh lime juice

Directions:

1. Bring 2 1/4 cups water, the coconut milk, carrots and onion to a boil in a 10-in. skillet.
2. Add shrimp, ramen noodles and snow peas; press down to submerge.
3. Bring to a simmer and, stirring to break up noodles, simmer 2 to 3 minutes until shrimp are cooked through.
4. Remove skillet from heat; stir in reserved seasoning packet, cilantro and lime juice.
5. Serve immediately.

Ramen Coconut Curry Shrimp

Ingredients:

2 package ramen noodles soup mix (any flavor)
½ cup light coconut milk
⅓ cup creamy peanut butter
2 tbsp. fresh lime juice
¼ tsp. red pepper flakes (optional)
1 lb. cooked, cleaned, peeled and deveined large shrimp
½ 1/2 seedless cucumber
4 scallions
Lime wedges, for serving

Directions:

1. Bring 4 cups water to a boil in a large skillet.
2. Break each package of noodles into 4 sections; add to boiling water (save seasoning packets for another use).
3. Cover skillet, remove from heat and let stand 5 minutes.
4. Meanwhile, in a large bowl, whisk together the coconut milk, peanut butter, lime juice and red pepper (if using).
5. Drain noodles.
6. Add them to the bowl with the dressing along with the shrimp, cucumber and scallions and toss to combine.
7. Serve with lime wedges, if desired.

Ramen Asian Meatball Soup

Ingredients:

8 oz. Lean Ground Beef
1/4 cup plain dry bread crumbs
W1 large egg, egg white only
1 tbsp. minced fresh ginger
1/2 tbsp. lite soy sauce
2 tsp. minced garlic
1 bag broccoli florets and baby carrots mix

Meatball Directions:

1. Mix ingredients until blended.
2. Place on wax paper; pat into a 6-in. square.
3. Cut in thirty-six 1-in. squares.
4. Bring 5 cups water to a gentle boil in a 4- to 5-qt pot.
5. Cut carrots in half diagonally.
6. Add carrots to boiling water, cover and cook 4 to 5 minutes until almost tender.
7. Add meatballs to pot, 1 at a time.
8. Stir in contents of noodle seasoning packets and the broccoli.
9. Reduce heat, cover and simmer 6 to 7 minutes until vegetables are tender.

Soup Directions:

1. Break each block of noodles in 4 pieces.
2. Add to soup and cook, stirring to separate strands, about 1 minute.
3. Stir in sugar snap peas and boil gently 2 minutes or until noodles are tender and peas turn bright green.
4. Stir in sesame oil; remove from heat. Garnish servings with scallions.

Ramen Vegetable Primavera

Ingredients:

1 bag frozen mixed vegetables (asparagus, carrots and cauliflower)
3 package any flavor ramen noodle soup
2 cup water
1 package French onion spreadable cheese
1 jar sliced pimientos

Directions:

1. Bring a half-filled 4- to 6-quart pot of water to boil.
2. Add frozen vegetables and return to a boil.
3. Add noodles and cook, stirring occasionally, 3 minutes or until vegetables and noodles are tender.
4. Drain in a colander.
5. Place pot over medium heat.
6. Add water, the seasoning packets and cheese; stir until smooth.
7. Add noodles, vegetables and pimientos; stir 3 minutes until hot and evenly coated.

Ramen Asian Shrimp and Noodle Soup

Ingredients:

8 cup water

4 package any flavor ramen noodle soup

12 oz. frozen, cooked, peeled and deveined medium shrimp

1 tsp. dark Oriental sesame oil

1/4 tsp. crushed red pepper

1/2 cup chopped scallions

1/3 cup grated carrots

4 Lime wedges

Directions:

1. Bring water to a boil in a 3- to 4-quart pot.
2. Break up noodles, add to pot and cook 3 minutes, stirring occasionally, or until tender.
3. Remove from heat.
4. Immediately stir in shrimp, seasoning packets, oil and crushed pepper.
5. Let stand 1 minute.
6. Sprinkle scallions and carrots over top.
7. Serve with lime wedges on the side.

Ramen Ricotta Frittata

Ingredients:

2 cup frozen green peas
3 package any flavor ramen noodle soup
1 container part-skim ricotta cheese
3 large eggs
1/2 cup milk
1/2 cup Grated Parmesan cheese
1/4 tsp. Pepper
1 can chunky tomatoes

Directions:

1. Heat oven to 400 degrees F.
2. Lightly grease a 13 x 9-inch baking dish.
3. Bring a half-filled 4- to 6-quart pot of water to boil.
4. Add frozen peas and return to a boil.
5. Break up noodles as directed on package and add to pot.
6. Cook 3 minutes, stirring occasionally, or until noodles and peas are tender.
7. Drain in a colander.
8. Meanwhile stir ricotta, eggs, milk, Parmesan, pepper and the 2 seasoning packets in a large bowl until blended.
9. Stir in noodles and peas.
10. Transfer mixture to prepared baking dish and spread evenly.
11. Bake about 20 minutes or until set.
12. Heat tomatoes in a saucepan or microwave until hot.
13. Spoon over frittata.
14. Cut in squares to serve.

Mongolian Beef Ramen Noodles

Ingredients:

1 1/2 lb. flank steak
1/4 cup cornstarch
1/4 cup vegetable oil
1 green bell pepper, sliced into thin strips
8 oz. dry ramen noodles
3 green onions, chopped

Sauce Ingredients:

2 tbsp. sesame oil
3/4 cup soy sauce, low sodium
2/3 cup brown sugar
1 1/4 cup chicken broth
4 cloves garlic, minced
1/4 tsp red pepper flakes

Directions:

1. Slice the flank steak into small thin pieces against the grain.
2. In a large ziploc bag add the starch and the beef to it.
3. Close the ziploc bag and shake really well until each pieces is coated with cornstarch.
4. In a non stick skillet heat the oil.
5. When the oil is hot, add beef and cook until browned.
6. It will take 2 or 3 batches because you don't want the steak pieces to stick to each other.
7. Also if you need more oil after the batch feel free to add more.
8. Remove beef from skillet to a plate and empty the oil from the skillet.

9. Add the bell pepper to the skillet and sauté it for a couple minutes just until it gets soft.
10. Remove the pepper from the skillet to a plate and set aside.
11. In that same skillet add sauce ingredients, the sesame oil, soy sauce, brown sugar, garlic, chicken broth and red pepper flakes.
12. Stir and cook over medium heat until sauce thickens a bit and reduces by about a quarter. It took me about 10 minutes until the sauce thickened and reduced. You don't want to reduce it too much because you need more sauce for the noodles.
13. In the meantime cook the ramen noodles according to package instructions.
14. Return the beef and bell pepper to the skillet and toss in the sauce.
15. Add the cooked ramen noodles to the skillet and toss everything together.
16. Top with green onions and serve.

Ramen Shrimp Lo Mein

Ingredients:

1 large white onion, diced
2 stalks celery, diced
1 large zucchini, quartered and then diced
1 bell pepper, diced
3 pkgs. oriental ramen noodles
2 pounds uncooked shrimp, shelled and de-veined

Directions:

1. In a large pan on medium high heat, add 2 tbsps. sunflower seed oil until shimmery.
2. Add onion, pepper and celery until slightly soft.
3. Add zucchini and cook until all vegetables are browned.
4. Add 8 oz. of water, noodles and spice packets from ramen pkgs., cover.
5. After about 6 minutes, check to see if noodles have softened- not enough to be ready, but enough to move around the pan without breaking them.
6. Stir around pan and add shrimp.
7. Cook for another 5-8 minutes, until shrimp are a nice, even pink- tossing as it cooks to ensure even heat.
8. Top with siracha, green onions, or anything you typically like with lo mein!

Ramen Sesame Peanut Butter Noodles

Ingredients:

6 oz. ramen noodles without the flavor packet
2 tbsp. pure sesame oil
1 1/2 tbsp. peanut butter
2 tbsp. honey
2 tbsp. soy sauce
1 1/2 tbsp. rice vinegar
1 garlic clove, minced
1/2 tsp. grated fresh ginger root
Optional Garnish: 3 sliced green onions and 1½ tsp. sesame seeds

Directions:

1. Cook and drain the noodles according to the package directions.
2. In a medium bowl, add the sesame oil, peanut butter, honey, soy sauce, rice vinegar, garlic, and ginger.
3. Whisk until well combined. The peanut butter should completely break down to create a smooth sauce.
4. Pour the sauce over the hot noodles.
5. Toss to coat.
6. Optional:
7. top each serving with 1 sliced green onion and 1/2 tsp. of sesame seeds.

Shrimp Wonton Miso Ramen

Ingredients:

2 pkgs. Ramen, miso flavored
4 oz. peeled and deveined shrimp
1/2 tsp. sesame oil
1/8 tsp. salt
1/2 tsp. cornstarch
10 wonton wrappers
1/4 cup boiled corn kernels
1 tbsp. chopped scallions

Directions:

1. Cut the shrimp into small pieces.
2. Add the sesame oil, salt and cornstarch, stir to mix well.
3. Add 1 tsp. of the shrimp filling onto the center of a wonton wrapper.
4. Wet your index finger with water and trace the outer corners of the wonton wrapper.
5. Fold, pinch and enclose the opening to form the wonton.
6. Repeat the same to make 10 wontons.
7. Heat up a small pot of water and bring it to boil.
8. Drop the wontons into the pot. As soon as they float to the top, remove them with a slotted spoon or strainer.
9. Set aside.
10. To make each bowl of ramen, boil two cups of water in the same pot.
11. Add the noodles and cook for 4 minutes or until al dente.
12. Meanwhile, empty the flavor pouch in a serving bowl.
13. Remove the noodles from heat and pour the water into the bowl first and mix well with a pair of chopsticks.
14. Add the noodles into the bowl and mix again.

15. Add the wontons, corns, and scallions as the toppings.

Kung Pao Ramen

Ingredients:

3 tbsps. canola oil
1 pound boneless, skinless chicken breasts (about 2-3), cubed
1 red bell pepper, cored and sliced thin
1/2 cup roasted unsalted peanuts
3 garlic cloves, finely minced
1 tbsp. grated fresh ginger
1/2 tsp. red pepper flakes
3 1/2 cups low-sodium chicken broth
4 (3 oz.) package ramen noodles, discard seasoning packets
2 tbsps. hoisin sauce
1 tbsp. rice vinegar
2 tsps. toasted sesame oil
4 scallions (green onions), sliced thin

Directions:

1. In a 12-inch nonstick skillet, heat 2 tbsps. of the canola oil over medium to medium-high heat until it is hot and rippling.
2. Season the chicken lightly with salt and pepper.
3. Add the cubed chicken to the pan in a single layer and cook, stirring occasionally, until the chicken is browned and cooked through, 5-7 minutes.
4. Remove the chicken to a medium bowl.
5. Add the last tbsp. of oil to the skillet and heat until hot and rippling.
6. Add the red bell pepper and the peanuts and cook until the pepper is softened, 2 to 3 minutes.
7. Remove the mixture into the bowl with the chicken, trying to leave as much oil as possible behind in the skillet.

8. Add the garlic, ginger and red pepper flakes to the remaining oil in the skillet and cook over medium heat, stirring constantly, for about 30 seconds to 1 minutes.
9. Stir in the chicken broth. Break the bricks of ramen into small chunks and add them to the skillet.
10. Bring the mixture to a simmer and cook, tossing the ramen constantly with tongs to separate, until ramen is just tender but there is still a bit of liquid in the pan, about 2-4 minutes.
11. Stir in the hoisin sauce, vinegar, and sesame oil and continue to simmer until the sauce is slightly thickened, about 1 minute.
12. Stir in the chicken, peppers and peanuts.
13. Sprinkle with green onions before serving.

Spicy Shrimp Ramen Noodle Bowl

Ingredients:

for the guacamole sauce
1 avocado, peeled and cubed (discard the pit)
2/3 cup canned coconut milk, well-shaken
juice from 1/2 fresh lime (the other half will be used for the shrimp)
juice from 1/2 fresh lemon (optional, but adds brightness)
1 scallion, roughly chopped
1 heaping tbsp. roughly chopped cilantro leaves and stems
1 tsp. chopped garlic (about 1 medium to large clove)
1 tsp. chopped jalapeno or serrano pepper (seeds removed)
1/2 tsp. kosher salt
for the shrimp
1 tbsp., plus 1 tsp., olive oil
1 pound medium-large raw shrimp, peeled, deveined, rinsed, and patted dry
1 tsp. southwest seasoning blend or chipotle chili powder (I used Mrs. Dash's Southwest Chipotle Blend)
1/2 tsp. pimenton (smoked paprika)
juice from 1/2 fresh lime
big pinch of kosher salt
for the noodle bowl
3 pkgs. ramen noodles (discard the flavor packets)
1 tbsp. chopped cilantro leaves
1 tbsp. chopped dill leaves
1 cup cherry tomatoes, sliced in half
1 small or mini cucumber, sliced
Cooked bacon bits for garnish (optional)

Directions:

1. for the guacamole sauce

2. Add all sauce ingredients to a blender or food processor and puree.
3. The sauce will be thick - thin with additional lime or lemon juice or water until it just reaches a pourable consistency. Taste, and season with additional salt, if necessary.
4. Set aside.
5. for the shrimp
6. Heat 1 tbsp. of olive oil in a large skillet over medium heat until the oil shimmers.
7. Toss the shrimp with 1 tsp. of olive oil, plus the remainder of the marinade ingredients.
8. Add the shrimp and sauté on one side for several minutes.
9. Flip each shrimp, and continue cooking until opaque, pink, and plump.
10. Remove from heat and set aside.
11. for the ramen noodle bowl
12. Prepare the ramen noodles according to package directions.
13. Drain, and let cool for several minutes.
14. Transfer to a large mixing or serving bowl.
15. Pour in about 3/4ths of the guacamole sauce and a big pinch each of cilantro and dill. Use tongs to gently toss the herbs and noodles with the sauce.
16. Gentle fold in the tomatoes and cucumbers.
17. Top with the shrimp, more herbs, a big drizzle of guacamole sauce, and the bacon bits.

Cacio e Pepe Ramen

Ingredients:

1 cup water
1 tbsp olive oil
2 tbsp unsalted butter
1 pkg. instant ramen noodles, spice packets discarded
1 cup cheese Parmesan
Fresh ground pepper

Directions:

1. Add water, olive oil, butter, and a few grinds of fresh pepper in a pan over medium heat.
2. Add enough butter to melt everything together.
3. Add cheese and stir.
4. When combined, add the noodles into the liquid and agitate them, 3-4 minutes.

Ramen Mi Goreng

Ingredients:

1 French shallot, thinly sliced
1 tbsp. kecap manis aka Indonesian sweet soy sauce
1 tbsp. ketchup or Sriracha
A dash of white pepper
3 drops of sesame oil
1 pinch of salt or soy sauce
2 packet of instant noodles (discard the enclosed seasoning packets)
2 tbsps. cooking oil
1/2 tbsp. shallot oil

Directions:

1. Thinly slice a French shallot.
2. Pat the sliced shallot with a paper towel to absorb excess moisture before pan frying.
3. Add cooking oil and shallot over medium flame.
4. When the shallot starts to sizzle, lower the flame to low and fry until golden brown.
5. Set aside in a bowl to cool.
6. In a bowl, add shallot oil, sesame oil, 1/2 tbsp. tomato sauce, kecap manis, white pepper and salt and mix until well combine.
7. Set aside
8. Cook noodles in boiling water according to package instructions.
9. Once cooked, toss the noodles with the sauce until well mix.
10. Sprinkle the fried shallots just before serving.
11. If desired, top with a sunny-side up egg and vegetables of your choice.

Avocado & Cherry Tomato Ramen Noodle Bowl

Ingredients:

for the lemon basil vinaigrette
1 heaping tsp. lemon zest (from about one large lemon)
2 tsps. minced lemon basil (or 1 1/2 tsps. sweet basil)
2 tbsps. lemon juice (from large lemon or two small)
2 tbsps. white wine vinegar
2 tbsps. extra virgin olive oil
1 tbsp. honey or agave
1/2 tsp. kosher salt (plus more as necessary, to taste)
for the noodle bowls
3 pkgs. ramen noodles, flavor packets discarded
1 tbsp. extra virgin olive oil
1 avocado, diced
1 pint cherry tomatoes, sliced into disks or quartered wedges
1 tbsp. lemon basil or sweet basil, minced

Directions:

1. Prepare the vinaigrette
2. Add all ingredients to a small mixing bowl and whisk well.
3. Set aside for at least a half hour, if possible, to let the flavors meld.
4. Taste, and add more salt if needed, one pinch at a time.
5. Prepare the noodle bowls
6. Bring a medium pot of water to boil.
7. Add the ramen noodles and reduce heat slightly to maintain an active simmer without boiling over.
8. Cook for three minutes (or according to package directions).
9. Drain in a colander and set aside to cool to room temperature (this takes just a few minutes).

10. When the ramen noodles have cooled, toss them with one tbsp. of olive oil plus two tbsps. of the vinaigrette.
11. Divide the noodles evenly between two entree-sized bowls.
12. Top each bowl with half of the sliced tomatoes and avocados, and drizzle the remaining vinaigrette evenly over each. Garnish with minced basil.

Creamy Ramen with Bacon

Ingredients:

1 pkg. Ramen instant noodles,
2 strips bacon
1/4 of a red onion
1/3 cup cream

Directions:

1. Cook Ramen according to package directions without the flavor packet.
2. Drain.
3. Cook the bacon and red onion together in a pan.
4. Once the onions are cooked down and the bacon is cooked to your liking.
5. Add cream.
6. Add the Ramen spice pack and let it simmer on low for a few minutes.
7. The cream will start to thicken.
8. Add the Ramen noodles.

Teriyaki Chow Mein

Ingredients:

1 pkg. ramen noodles, beef flavor
1-14 oz. can beef broth
1/4 cup teriyaki sauce
1/2 stalk celery, sliced to 1/4 inch
1/2 cup broccoli, finely chopped
1-3.5 oz. can mushrooms, sliced and drained
2 med. green onions, sliced
2 cloves garlic, minced
1/2 tsp. celery salt
4 oz. flank steak, cut into 1/4 inch slices
1-1/2 tbsp. cornstarch

Directions:

1. In a medium wok, add the beef broth and teriyaki sauce and heat to medium-high, bring to a slight boil.
2. Add the celery, broccoli, mushrooms, green onions, garlic and celery salt.
3. Bring to a boil and then reduce heat to medium and simmer for 8-10 minutes.
4. In a skillet, add the flank steak and sauté until there is no pink.
5. When the meat is done and the time is done on the wok, add the meat and the ramen noodle and simmer for 3 minutes.
6. When done, add a little water to the cornstarch, mix, and then add it to the wok, off the heat, return to heat, lower heat to low and simmer for 5 minutes or until broth thickens.
7. Serve.

Beef & Broccoli Ramen

Ingredients:

1 package beef ramen noodles
2 cups water
1 tbsp. oil
3/4 pound beef sirloin cubed
1 onion cut in wedges
2 cups broccoli, cut up
1/2 tsps. garlic powder
1 can cream of broccoli soup
1/4 cup water
1 tbsp. soy sauce

Directions:

1. Cook noodles according to package directions and drain.
2. Add seasoning packet.
3. Brown beef in oil with garlic powder.
4. Add onion and broccoli.
5. Cook over medium heat until tender.
6. Add soup concentrate, 1/4 cup water and soy sauce.
7. Simmer ten minutes.
8. Serve over noodles.

Ramen Beef Tomato Noodle Skillet

Ingredients:

1 package of Ramen Noodles crunched up
2 cans of tomatoes
1 can of corn (not creamed)
1 lb ground beef

Directions:

1. Brown the beef and drain.
2. Add the tomatoes, corn, and noodles.
3. Make sure to add the seasoning package to the meal.
4. Bring to boil.
5. Cover, stirring occasionally.
6. Bring the meal until most of the tomato sauce is evaporated and the noodles are soft.

Ramen with Veggies

Ingredients:

4 pkgs. of ramen, any flavor
1 lb. of chicken, beef or tofu
1 Cup frozen vegetables
Shredded cheese
Duck sauce
Soy sauce

Directions:

1. Sauté meat until done.
2. Cook Ramen in enough water to cover.
3. Add Frozen Veggies to Ramen 1 minute before done.
4. Drain a bit of the water but not all so that it is like a chunky soup.
5. Add flavor packets.
6. Top with shredded cheese,   duck sauce and soy sauce to taste.

Cheesy Chili Ramen

Ingredients:

1 pkg. chicken flavored Ramen noodles, flavor packets discarded
1 cube chipotle flavored bouillion
2 tsps. cheddar powder (from instant mac & cheese or popcorn seasoning)
2 tsps. butter
1 green onion, diced

Directions:

1. Combine all ingredients to a microwave safe dish.
2. Add water.
3. Microwave 3 minutes.
4. Top with green onion.

Cheesy Ramen Meat Pie

Ingredients:

2 bags beef ramen noodles
1 can (25 oz.) chili
1/4 bag nacho cheese tortilla chips (Doritos)
1/4 cup jalapeno pepper, diced
1 tbsp. chili powder
1 metal pie pan
7 - 8 slices processed cheese (American, Velveeta, etc.)

Directions:

1. Boil three cups of water.
2. Add the noodles and cook, about 5 minutes.
3. Drain.
4. Preheat oven to 350 degrees F.
5.   Heat chili in small sauce pan just until hot.
6. Add the seasoning packets to noodles.
7. Lightly butter the pie tin.
8. Add chips to the pie tin until the bottom is covered.
9. Add enough noodles to cover the chips.
10. Add some chilli on top of the noodles.
11. Add the peppers and chilli powder.
12. Add some cheese and more chips.
13. Add more chips.
14. Repeat layering until all ingredients are gone making sure the last two layers are cheese and then chips on top.
15. Cook about 10 or 15 minutes.

Chile Ramen

Ingredients:

1 package of beef ramen
1 can chili
shredded cheddar
1 cup nacho cheese tortilla chips (Doritos), crushed
1/4 cup onion, chopped

Directions:

1. Cook noodles as indicated on package
2. Drain all water from noodles
3. Add can of chili, onions, and Doritos.
4. Stir.
5. Top with cheese.

Faux Pho Ramen

Ingredients:

1 tbs. canola oil
1.5 lbs. flank steak, very thinly sliced against the grain
4 cups beef broth
4 cups chicken broth
1 cup water
4 packets of ramen noodles (discard spice packet)
2 tbs. soy sauce
mung bean sprouts
chopped basil
Sriracha

Directions:

1. Heat oil in a large pot over high heat.
2. Add beef and cook until just browned, stirring often. About 3 minutes.
3. Transfer to plate using tongs, preserving juices in the pot.
4. Add bok choy to pot and cook till wilted, stirring often.
5. Add broths and water.
6. Stir and cover, bring to a boil.
7. Reduce heat to simmer.
8. Add ramen and soy sauce.
9. Simmer until noodles become soft.
10. Re-add beef.
11. Cook until hot.
12. Serve with chopped basil, bean sprouts and sriracha.

Hamburger Ramen

Ingredients:

1 pkg. beef ramen noodles
2 cups water
1/2 lb. ground beef

Directions:

1. Brown beef.
2. Drain fat.
3. Season with half of the seasoning packet.
4. Cook noodles according to package directions and drain.
5. Mix together.

Taco Ramen

Ingredients:

1 pkg. ramen noodles, beef flavor
1 (15 oz.) can diced tomatoes
1/2 cup water
2 tbsps. taco seasoning mix
1/2 cup canned chicken
1/2 cup sweet corn
1/2 cup cheddar cheese, shredded
1/4 cup cilantro

Directions:

1. In a large pot, bring ramen noodles, half of the ramen beef seasoning packet, diced tomatoes, and water to a boil.
2. Cook until the noodles are softened, about 3 minutes.
3. Remove from heat and pour into two serving bowls.
4. Sprinkle remaining ramen beef seasoning over the canned chicken.
5. Place half of the chicken on top of the ramen in each bow.
6. Heat corn in a small, microwave safe bowl until warm, about 1 minute.
7. Place on top of ramen in each bowl.
8. Top each bowl with cheddar cheese and cilantro.

Taco Ramen Salad

Ingredients:

1 pkg. beef ramen noodles
1/2 lb. ground beef
1 small tomato, chopped
1/2 cup onion chopped
1 cup cheddar cheese, shredded
Thousand Island dressing to taste

Directions:

1. Cook noodles according to package directions and drain.
2. Brown beef
3. and drain.
4. Stir in half the seasoning packet.
5. Mix all ingredients together.
6. Add dressing.

Ramen Lasagna

Ingredients:

58 oz. Tomato Sauce
12 oz. Tomato Paste
1 tbs. salt
2 tsp. pepper
2 tbs. dried onion
1 tbs. dried oregano
1 tbs. dried parsley
2 tsp garlic powder
1 lb. Italian sausage
6 packets of ramen noodles (discard seasoning packets)
23 oz. ricotta cheese
2 cups grated mozzarella

Directions:

1. Combine tomato paste and tomato sauce with salt, pepper, onion, oregano, parsley and garlic powder.
2. Stir until there are no lumps.
3. Remove skin from Italian sausage and cook on med/high heat, or until it is fully browned.
4. Remove from heat and set aside.
5. Line the bottom of a greased casserole dish with a thin layer of tomato sauce.
6. Drop a block of dried noodles into boiling water.
7. Wait until the underside is just done and then flip the noodle patty over to finish cooking.
8. Remove from the pot with a slotted spatula and unfold them on to a plate so they resembled a long strip and slide them in rows on top of the sauce.
9. Repeat until sauce is completely covered by noodles, three pkgs. of noodles.
10. Cover the noodle layer with the ricotta.
11. Distribute sausage on top of ricotta.

12. Cover sausage with half of the remaining tomato sauce.
13. Place three more noodle strips on top of sauce.
14. Cover noodles with sauce and top with shredded cheese.
15. Place into 350 degree oven and bake for 40 minutes, or until it is brown and bubbly.

Ramen Kibbee

Ingredients:

1 pkg. of Ramen, beef flavored
1 lb. ground meat, uncooked
1 tsp. cumin seeds
1 tsp. seal salt
1/2 cup diced onion
1/8 cup extra virgin olive oil

Directions:

1. Brown ground beef and drain
2. In a large bowl, put in ground meat, ramen including seasoning packet, cumin, salt, onion and olive oil.
3. Blend well with your hands, breaking the ramen noodles and mixing all ingredients well.
4. Place mixture in an ungreased meatloaf pan.
5. Bake at 350 degrees F for one hour.

Sloppy Joe Ramen

Ingredients:

3 pkgs. ramen noodles any flavor (don't need flavor packs)
4 tbsp. sloppy joe seasoning mix
1 lb. ground beef
2 cans (48 oz.) diced tomatoes with juice
1 cup water
1 cup bell peppers, chopped

Directions:

1. Brown beef and drain.
2. In large pot with lid add water, tomatoes, and sloppy joe seasoning.
3. Mix well, and bring to a boil.
4. Add the ramen noodles (broken up some), beef and bell pepper.
5. Reduce heat to simmer and cover with lid.
6. Cook for 20-30 min. watching closely.
7. Add more water if necessary.

Spicy Beef Ramen Noodle Soup

1 tbsp. roasted garlic in olive oil
1 can diced tomatoes with jalepeno's
1 can beef broth
1 can chicken broth with roasted garlic
1 cup medium to hot salsa
1 pkg. beef ramen noodles

Directions:

1. Combine everything in a medium saucepan.
2. Bring to boil for 3 minutes.

Pineapple Meatballs Ramen

Ingredients:

2 pkgs. of ramen noodles
1/2 lb. of ground beef
1/2 cup of pineapple, sliced
1/2 cup of red peppers, sliced
2-3 tbsp. of Worcestershire sauce
1-2 tsp. of garlic powder
1 tsp. of salt
1/3 cup of vegetable oil
4 cups of water

Directions:

1. The noodles:
2. Put 4 cups of water in a cooking pot and bring to a boil.
3. Once the water is boiling add your ramen noodles.
4. Wait 2-3 minutes until the noodles are tender and separated.
5. Take off the water with the strainer.
6. The recipe:
7. Mix the ground beef, the Worcestershire sauce, the garlic powder and the salt together.
8. Make the meatballs.
9. Add the vegetable oil in a cooking pan and brown the meatballs.
10. Reduce heat and simmer for 10 minutes
11. When the meatballs are almost ready add the pineapples and the red peppers cook for another 5 minutes.
12. When your meatballs are fully cooked and the pineapples/peppers are ready, put everything in a large plate.

Spicy Ramen Pasta

Ingredients:

2 cups of Prego mushroom sauce
1 1/2 cups Italian sausage
1/3 cup diced green pepper
1 tbsp of Parmesan cheese
1/2 tsp diced garlic
1/2 tsp onion powder
1/2 tsp hot sauce
1 packet of Ramen beef flavoring

Directions:

1. Cook Italian sausage and add in beef flavoring
2. Add all other ingredients to sauce
3. Bring water to a boil and cook Ramen noodles
4. Add noodles to sauce
5. Sprinkle Parmesan cheese on top

Teriyaki Ramen Chow Mein

Ingredients:

1 pkg. ramen noodles, beef flavor
1-14 oz. can Beef broth
1/4 cup Teriyaki sauce
1/2 stalk Celery, sliced to 1/4 inch
1/2 cup Broccoli, finely chopped
1-3.5 oz. can Mushrooms, sliced and drained
2 medium Green onions, sliced
2 cloves Garlic, minced
1/2 tsp Celery salt
4 oz Flank steak, cut into 1/4 inch slices
1-1/2 tbsp Cornstarch

Directions:

1. In a medium wok, add the beef broth and teriyaki sauce and heat to medium-high, bring to a slight boil.
2. Add the celery, broccoli, mushrooms, green onions, garlic and celery salt.
3. Bring to a boil and then reduce heat to medium and simmer for 8-10 minutes.
4. In a skillet, add the flank steak and sauté until there is no pink.
5. When the meat is done and the time is done on the wok, add the meat and the ramen noodle and simmer for 3 minutes.
6. When done, add a little water to the cornstarch, mix, and then add it to the wok, off the heat, return to heat, lower heat to low and simmer for 5 minutes or until broth thickens.

Ramen Mix

Ingredients:

1 pkg. of ramen noodles, season packet discarded
1 cup of salsa
1 cup sliced pepperoni or ham strips
1 tbsp. pickle relish
1 tsp. mustard

Directions:

1. Make ramen according to package directions.
2. Drain noodles.
3. Mix everything together and enjoy!

Bacon and Egg Ramen Burrito

Ingredients:

1 pkg. Pork Ramen
Bacon
1 egg
Hot sauce
Flour tortilla
Cheese, optional

Directions:

1. Boil 2 cups of water &
2. Cook ramen for 3 minutes.
3. In a skillet over med heat, scramble eggs.
4. Add hot sauce and pieces of cooked bacon.
5. Drain the Ramen.
6. Put the well drained noodles on a flour tortilla, top with egg and bacon mix.
7. Add cheese if desired.
8. Wrap, return to hot skillet for 30 seconds to melt cheese & heat the burrito.
9. Serve and enjoy!

Sausage Egg Ramen Burrito

Ingredients:

1 pkg. pork ramen
sausage
1 egg
Hot sauce
1 flour tortilla
Cheese, optional

Directions:

1. Boil 2 cups of water & Cook ramen for 3 minutes. While ramen is cooking, in a skillet over medium heat, scramble eggs with hot sauce and sausage.
2. Drain the Ramen.
3. Put the well drained noodles on a flour tortilla, top with egg/sausage mix.
4. Add cheese if desired.
5. Wrap, return to hot skillet for 30 seconds to melt cheese & heat the burrito.

Breakfast Ramen

Ingredients:

1 pkg. oriental ramen
green onion
3 tbsp. butter
2 eggs
1/2 tsp. soy sauce
1/2 tsp. sesame oil
1/2 tsp. baking powder

Directions:

1. Cook the ramen in a couple cups of boiling water for 3 minutes.
2. While ramen is cooking whisk eggs, onions, 1/2 of the ramen flavoring, soy sauce, sesame oil, and baking powder in small bowl.
3. Drain Ramen.
4. Heat butter in a skillet then add cooked ramen & sauté 3 minutes.
5. Pour egg mixture over the noodles in the skillet, cook until set.
6. Flip the noodle/egg combo over to finish cooking until the eggs are completely done.
7. Serve with extra soy sauce if desired.

Parmesan Ramen

Ingredients:

1 package any flavor ramen noodles
2 cups water
1/4 cup parmesan cheese

Directions:

1. Cook noodles according to package directions and drain.
2. Sprinkle with parmesan.

Peanut Butter Ramen Snack

Ingredients:

5 tbsp. peanut butter
1 pkg. ramen noodles
1/4 cup melted chocolate

Directions:

1. Spoon 5 tbsps. of peanut butter into a small bowl
2. Keep 1 Cup of ramen noodles in the package and hit either with hand or utensil to break off into about 10 chunks
3. Take each chunk of broken ramen and coat it in peanut butter in the bowl.
4. Place each coated chunk onto cookie sheet
5. Melt 1/4 cup of chocolate and drizzle over peanut butter.
6. Chill in freezer for 15 minutes.

Ramen Alfredo

Ingredients:

8 oz. heavy cream
1 tbsp. butter
2 packs ramen
Salt and pepper to taste
1/4 cup parmesan cheese
1 tsp. of garlic powder
1 tsp. onion powder

Directions:

1. Start by boiling the ramen as bag says.
2. When done strain pasta use the same pot over a med heat and put the cream and start reducing it.
3. Add all seasonings and continue to reduce. Let it reduce for 5 mins.
4. Add cooked ramen and cheese and let cook for 1 min.

Lemon and Lime Ramen

Ingredients:

1 pack of chicken flavor ramen noodles
1 lemon
1 lime
2 tsps. adobo seasoning
1 tsp. Cajun spice

Directions:

1. Boil 1 pack of ramen noodles in 2 cups of water for 2 minutes
2. After 2 minutes, remove noodles from heat
3. Squeeze as much juice as possible from the lemon and lime
4. Pour out water used to boil noodles and replace with juice from the lemon and lime
5. Boil noodles in lemon and lime juice for 1 minute
6. Add Chicken flavoring pack, 2 tsps. of Adobo, and 1 tsp. of Cajun Spice
7. Stir together until everything looks nicely combined and remove from heat
8. Place everything into a bowl and serve while still hot

Tomato Ramen Soup

Ingredients:

1 pkg. ramen noodles, any flavor
2 cups water
1 can tomato soup

Directions:

1. Cook noodles according to package directions.
2. Do not drain.
3. Add the tomato soup concentrate.
4. Simmer five minutes.
5. Serve and enjoy!

Veggie Ramen

1 pkg. any flavor ramen noodles
2 cups water
1 cup mixed veggies (fresh, frozen or canned)

Directions:

1. Cook noodles according to package directions with the veggies and drain.
2. Add the seasoning packet.

Crab Ramen Tahini Salad

Dressing Ingredients:

2 tbsps. tahini
1/2 cup light soy sauce
1/4 cup rice vinegar
1/4 cup brown sugar, packed
2 seasoning packets from the ramen noodle pkgs.
1/4 tsp. ground ginger
1/4 tsp. garlic powder
1/2 cup toasted sesame oil
1/4 cup canola oil

Salad Ingredients:

2 (3-oz.) pkgs. shrimp-flavored ramen noodles, uncooked, crushed
1 (16-oz.) package cole slaw mix
1 small red bell pepper, julienned
1/2 cup thinly sliced scallions
1 (8-oz.) package imitation crab meat, diced
1/4 cup sliced almonds

Directions:

1. In a small bowl, combine the dressing ingredients in a bowl; whisk to combine.
2. In a large salad bowl, toss the ramen noodles, coleslaw mix, red pepper and scallions.
3. Top with imitation crab meat. Drizzle with dressing.
4. Garnish with sliced almonds.
5. Serve immediately or refrigerate.

Grilled Salmon & Noodle Dish

Ingredients:

8 oz. salmon fillet
olive oil
1 package Oriental Flavor Ramen noodles
12 baby carrots cut lengthwise into 4 pieces
1/4 cup chopped onion
1/4 cup slice red bell pepper
1 T. freshly grated ginger
1 tsp. lemon grass
1 tsp soy sauce
1/2 tsp. hot chili paste
1 T chopped fresh cilantro
1 tsp fresh lime juice

Directions:

1. Rub salmon with oil, grill over medium heat about 10 minutes or until done.
2. Cook ramen noodles according to package directions.
3. In a skillet sauté, carrots, onions & red bell pepper until crisp tender about 7 minutes.
4. Add ginger, lemon grass, soy sauce & hot chili paste cook 2 minutes, deglaze pan with 2 T liquid from Ramen noodles.
5. Remove from heat & stir in cilantro.
6. Place noodles on plate top with vegetables & salmon.
7. Drizzle salmon with lime juice.

Ramen Spicy Shrimp and Noodle Soup

Ingredients:

1 lb. shrimp
1 tbsp. lemon juice
1/4 tsp. chili powder
1/4 tsp. ground cumin
1/8 tsp. black pepper
5 cups water
2 pkgs. shrimp or oriental flavored ramen noodles (use only 1 packet of seasoning)
2 cups salsa
1 (15oz.) can black beans rinsed and drained
1 can corn
1 green onion thinly sliced

Directions:

1. Peel and devein shrimp.
2. In a medium bowl combine lemon juice chili powder, cumin, and pepper.
3. Add mixture to shrimp.
4. Toss to coat.
5. Let stand 20 minutes.
6. In a large sauce pan bring water to boil, stir in ramen flavor packet.
7. Break ramen noodles into pieces.
8. Add to saucepan.
9. Return to boil cook for 1 minute.
10. Add shrimp, salsa, beans, corn, and green onion heat though until shrimp turn pink.

Sweet and Sour Ramen Soup

Ingredients:

2 chicken breasts diced
1 cup chicken broth
Ramen noodles
1 cup water
4 tbsps. apple cider vinegar
4 tbsps. Bragg's liquid aminos
½ lemon in quarters with rind
1 clove garlic crushed and minced
2 tbsps. minced onion
Cayenne pepper to taste
Pinch of chili powder or red chili flakes
Salt and pepper to taste

Directions:

1. Boil lemon wedges with rind in 1 cup of water until pulp comes out of the
2. rind.
3. Scrape out additional pulp and juice.
4. Add the diced chicken, spices, ramen noodles, and chicken broth.
5. Simmer until cooked.
6. Serve and enjoy!

Tomato and onion Tuna Ramen

Ingredients:

1 pkg. ramen noodles, any flavor, seasoning packet discarded
1 can of condensed tomato soup,
1 can of water for soup
½ pouch tuna fish
1 small tomato, diced
1/4 cup of a white onion
1 clove of garlic
1 tsp. of fresh ginger
1 squirt of lime
Salt and pepper to taste

Directions:

1. Heat tomato soup and water for about a minute.
2. Add broken up ramen.
3. Cover and let simmer over low heat for about 3 minutes.
4. Add tuna, tomato, onion, garlic and ginger.
5. Stir and continue to cook for an additional minute.
6. Add lime, salt and pepper to taste just before serving.

Banana Coconut Ramen Pudding

Ingredients:

3 pkgs. ramen noodles, seasoning packets discarded
4 tbsps. unsalted butter, melted, plus more for greasing
2 large eggs
2/3 cup sugar
1 (14 oz.) can coconut milk
1/2 cup sour cream
1 1/2 tsps. almond extract
1/4 tsp. ground cardamom
1/4 tsp. anise seed, crushed
Salt
1/2 cup golden raisins
1/4 cup crystallized ginger, chopped
2 bananas, thinly sliced
1/4 cup shredded coconut
2 tbsps. sliced almonds

Directions:

1. Preheat the oven to 350F. Butter an 8-inch square baking dish; spread out the bananas in a layer on the bottom of the buttered dish.
2. Place the noodles in a bowl, cover with hot tap water and soak, flipping once, for 10 minutes; the noodles should pull apart easily.
3. Drain well; toss with the melted butter.
4. In a large bowl combine the eggs, sugar, coconut milk, sour cream, almond extract, cardamom, anise seed and a pinch of salt, whisking well until fully incorporated.
5. Stir in the noodles, raisins and ginger until combined.
6. Gently
7. Pour over the bananas in the prepared pan.

8. Sprinkle coconut and almonds over the top, Bake until golden brown and set, about 1 hour 10 minutes. Let cool for at least 1 hour before slicing.

Chocolatey Ramen

Ingredients:

1/2 stick of butter
1 package of ramen noodles
1/2 tsp. of vanilla extract
1 1/2 cups of semi-sweet chocolate chips
1 sheet of waxed paper

Directions:

1. Crush up the noodles into small bite sized pieces.
2. Melt the butter in a medium sauce pan on medium heat.
3. Add in the vanilla extract.
4. Mix in the chocolate chips.
5. Pour the chocolate mixture into a bowl.
6. Mix in the noodles and stir so that each noodle is well covered.
7. Place the noodle clusters onto a sheet of waxed paper.
8. Place into the fridge for approx. 10 minutes, or until each cluster is cooled off and ready
9. to eat. Enjoy!

Chocolate Peanut Butter Ramen Krispies

Ingredients:

1/2 cup creamy peanut butter
1/4 cup cocoa powder
1/2 cup corn syrup
3 pkgs. ramen noodle, any flavor

Directions:

1. Line an 8" square pan with foil.
2. Remove ramen noodles from package and place into a bowl. Save seasoning for another use.
3. Break noodles apart in to cereal size pieces.
4. In another bowl mix together the peanut butter, cocoa powder, and corn syrup.
5. Fold in ramen noodles and press in to foil lined bowl.
6. Place in fridge until firm.
7. Remove from pan by lifting the foil.
8. Cut into desired size. For a tasty and pepped up alteration,
9. add 1tsp instant coffee to peanut butter mixture.

Chocolate Ramen Cakes

Ingredients:

1 pkg. ramen noodles, crushed, seasoning packet discarded
2 t. oil
4 small dessert cupcakes
1/3 cup drained maraschino cherries
1 cup hot fudge sauce or chocolate syrup
1 banana, sliced

Directions:

1. Heat the oil in a small pan, sauté raw crushed ramen noodles until lightly browned.
2. Remove from heat.
3. In 2 bowls, place 2 cakes, top with cherries and sliced banana's and divide the toasted ramen noodles equally over the cakes.
4. Lavishly pour warm hot fudge sauce or chocolate syrup over the top, garnish with whipped cream if desired.
5. Serve and enjoy!

Chocolate Ramen Dessert

Ingredients:

1 pkg. any flavor ramen- crushed seasoning packet
discarded
1 cup brown sugar
Chocolate syrup
1 tsp vanilla
Powdered sugar

Directions:

1. Boil the ramen in 2 cups of hot water with 1 cup of
   brown sugar added to it for 3 1/2 minutes.
2. Remove from heat and drain 98% of the water (in other
   words, leave a tiny bit).
3. Add 1 tsp vanilla extract and approximately 1/4 cup
   chocolate syrup.
4. Sprinkle generously with powdered sugar & add a
   dollop of whipped cream.

Graham Cracker Ramen Cookies

Ingredients:

5 whole honey graham crackers
1 pkg. ramen noodles, seasoning packet discarded
1 cup semi-sweet chocolate chips
1 cup peanut butter
1 cup fruit loop cereal
1/2 c dried cranberries

Directions:

1. Break each graham cracker in half.
2. Melt the Chocolate in the microwave 20 seconds at a time.
3. Crush up Ramen noodles, transfer to a medium bowl.
4. Heat Peanut Butter in the microwave, until it is thinner in texture.
5. Mix melted chocolate, peanut butter and raw ramen in the bowl.
6. Line each graham cracker half with dried cranberries.
7. Spoon the chocolate mixture over the cranberries.
8. Garnish with fruit loop cereal

Ice Cream Ramen

Ingredients:

4 scoops vanilla ice cream
1/4 cup sliced almonds or other nuts
1 pkg ramen noodles, seasoning packet discarded
1/2cup honey
4 tbsp. chocolate syrup
2 tbsp. vegetable oil

Directions:

1. Sauté dry ramen noodles in oil until crisp.
2. Pour honey in pan and stir till lightly bubbles
3. Spoon 1/4 of ramen honey mixture over 1 Scoop of vanilla ice cream.
4. Sprinkle with almonds or other nuts
5. Drizzle with 1 tbsp. chocolate syrup

Jello Ramen Noodles

Ingredients:

1 pkg. of ramen noodles, crushed, seasoning packet discarded
1 pkg. of Jello
1 tbsp. of vegetable oil (canola)
1 cup of cold water
1 cup of hot water

Directions:

1. Heat oil in a small frying pan, once hot, add crushed raw ramen noodles.
2. Sauté until lightly browned, remove from heat.
3. In a separate bowl combine Jello and hot water, stir until dissolved.
4. Add 1 cup of cold water.
5. Mix until well blended, add ramen noodles.
6. Place in fridge to set.
7. Serve and enjoy!

Ramen Sugar Cookies

Ingredients:

2 3/4 cups all-purpose flour
1 tsp. baking soda
1/2 tsp. baking powder
1 cup butter, softened
1 1/2 cups white sugar
1 egg
1 tsp. vanilla extract
1 cup chocolate
1 pkg. of ramen noodles, chicken flavor
1 cup toasted almonds

Directions:

1. Preheat oven to 375 degrees F.
2. In a small bowl, stir together four, baking soda, and baking powder.
3. Set aside.
4. In a large bowl, cream together the butter and sugar until smooth.
5. Beat in egg and vanilla.
6. Gradually blend in the dry ingredients.
7. Roll the cookies dough out to a 1/4".
8. Slice the dough into small rectangles, about 2" long and 1" wide.
9. Place onto un-greased cookie sheet.
10. Bake 9 to 11 minute in the preheated oven, or until golden.
11. Let stand on cookie sheet two minutes before removing to cool on wire racks.
12. While the cookies cool, melt chocolate.

13. After the cookies have cooled, dip half the cookie in the melted chocolate and sprinkle toasted almonds and toasted Ramen noodles on the chocolate side of the cookie.
14. Sprinkle a pinch of some of the chicken seasoning on the chocolate side.

About the Author

Laura Sommers is **The Recipe Lady!**

She lives on a small farm in Baltimore County, Maryland and has a passion for all things domestic especially when it comes to saving money. She has a profitable eBay business and is a couponing addict. Follow her tips and tricks to learn how to make delicious meals on a budget, save money or to learn the latest life hack!

Follow her on Pinterest:

http://pinterest.com/therecipelady1

Visit the Recipe Lady's blog for even more great recipes:

http://the-recipe-lady.blogspot.com/

Visit her Amazon Author Page to see her latest books:

amazon.com/author/laurasommers

Follow the Recipe Lady on Facebook:

https://www.facebook.com/therecipegirl

Follow me on Twitter:

https://twitter.com/TheRecipeLady1

Other Books by Laura Sommers

- Recipe Hacks for Saltine Crackers
- Recipe Hacks for Canned Biscuits
- Recipe Hacks for Canned Soup
- Recipe Hacks for Beer
- Recipe Hacks for Peanut Butter
- Recipe Hacks for Potato Chips
- Recipe Hacks for Oreo Cookies
- Recipe Hacks for Cheese Puffs
- Recipe Hacks for Pasta Sauce
- Recipe Hacks for Canned Tuna Fish
- How to Shop for Penny Items

May all of your meals be a banquet
with good friends and good food.

Made in the USA
Las Vegas, NV
11 December 2022

61906909R00069